Praises for

"We are for anyone who is for Jesus...and Robin is for Jesus. In this resource she has used her creative talents to present the faith to children. May it be a blessing."
Dr. Stephen and Kellie Swisher (Copeland)

To:
From:

Kid Praise Party

Empowering Kids through Praise
Kingdom Kids Series #1

By Robin Bremer

Kid Praise Party
Empowering Kids through Praise
Kingdom Kids Series #1
By Robin Bremer
Published by Robin E. Bremer 2014
http://www.robinbremer.net
ALL RIGHTS RESERVED
No portion of this publication may be reproduced, stored in any electronic system or transmitted in any form or by any means, electronic, mechanical, photocopy, recording or otherwise, without the written permissions from the author and publisher. Brief quotations may be used in literary reviews. Unless otherwise noted, all scripture references are taken from the King James Version of the Holy Bible.
Copyright © 2014 Robin Bremer
All rights reserved.
ISBN-13: 978-1496044846
ISBN-10: 1496044843

ACKNOWLEDGMENTS

I want to thank the kids from Faith Community Church in Oklahoma for drawing the pictures included in this book. The pictures were great and I enjoyed teaching you and watching you learn how to praise with the flag, banners, veils, and ribbons. You were awesome and you will be used greatly of God.

KIDS PRAISE PARTY

Ps 63:1-4 is a great model of prayer and praise. We can pray this way: Oh God You are my God, I will look to you first. I want to feel Your presence, My spirit wants to know you. I feel so empty without you. I look for you at church to see your power and glory because your loving kindness is better than anything in life. I will say good things about you. I will lift my hands and praise you. I will get the answer to my prayer and I will be joyful.

Praising God is how we get God to visit us. Ps 100:4. We thank Him for all He has done for us. We praise by being thankful to Him because He is always GOOD. We praise God by saying what the Bible says about Him. When we praise He will always come to hear what you are saying about Him.

We can praise God by calling Him by some of His Names. We could say something like, Father God, I just praise you right now because you are My Lord God Almighty you are the Most High God My Lord and Master. You are My Lord. Here are some more Hebrew names for God. (Lord God Almighty) El Shaddai, (The Most High God) El Elyon (Lord, Master) Adonai, (Lord, Jehovah) Yahweh.

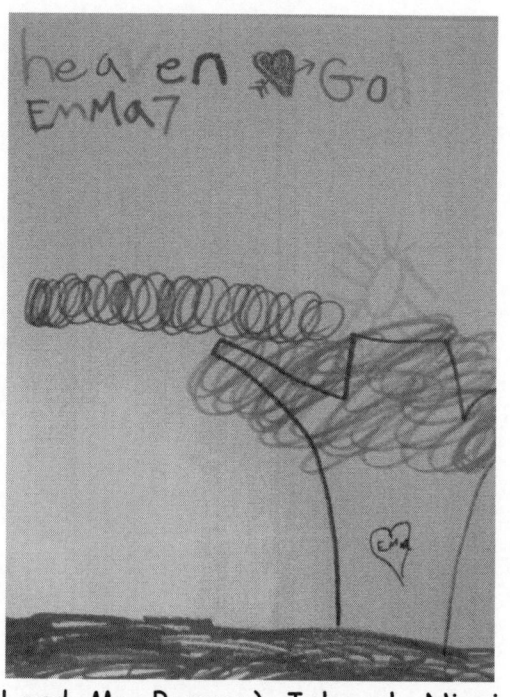

(The Lord My Banner) Jehovah Nissi, (The Lord My Shepherd) Jehovah-Raah, (The Lord That Heals) Jehovah Rapha, (The Lord Is There) Jehovah Shammah, (The Lord Our Righteousness) Jehovah Tsidkenu, (The Lord Will Provide) Jehovah Jireh, (The Lord Is Peace) Jehovah Shalom. You could praise like this, "Father God you are my Jehovah Jireh my provider. You provide everything I need. I thank you for providing my (fill in this blank with what you need) _____ that I need."

We show our praise and worship by shouting (Ps 35:27) or by bowing down or kneeling with an expecting attitude. We also praise God by telling others all the wonderful things He has done for us. We can praise God with our whole body when we praise Him in our dance.

We can praise God by dancing or with an instrument. Ps 150, Ps 57:8, Ps 22:3 When we sing to God or about God we are praising Him. 2 Ch 20:22 When we sing out of our spirit, instead of a written song we are praising God.

When we lift our hands we are praising God. The Bible tells us to lift our hands to God when we are praising Him.
Ps 141:2, 1 Tim 2:8, Ps 134:2

When we sing or say the word we can be praising God. Col 3:16. We can praise in tongues or in your Heavenly language.

Here are 7 words from the Bible that show us how to praise. Yadah: extending your hands. Towdah: extend hands in thanksgiving. Halal: to shine, boast, celebrate, to be foolish. Shabach: to shout loudly Ps 35:27. Barak: to Kneel to bless God, to bow down in an expecting attitude. Zamar: rejoicing, instrument. Tehillah: to sing praises. Ps 22:3 He inhabits praise.

We are to always praise at all times because God has a good answer for us. Heb 13:15. We can praise Him with words or in dance.

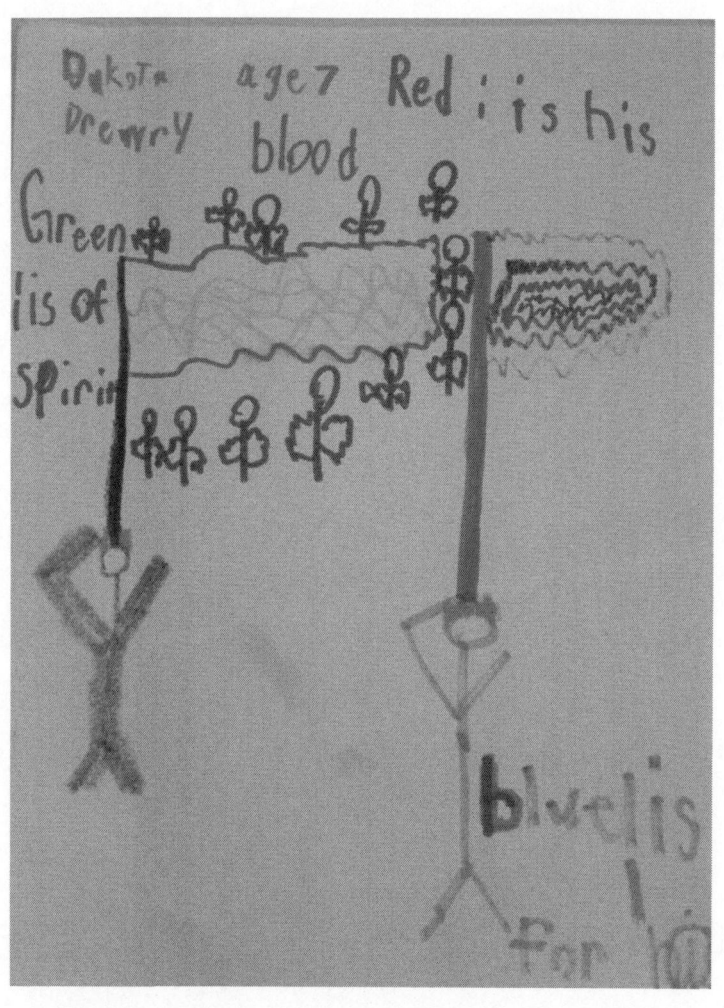

Praising God gives you strength and stops the enemy. Mat 21:16, Ps 8:2

We can praise Him with our words, songs, paintings, and dance! God comes and visit us when we praise Him.
Ps 22:3

God brings the answer to all our problems when we praise.
Ps 50:14-15,23

Praise brings you into Gods will and Gods will is for all good things to happen to you. 1 The 5:17-18

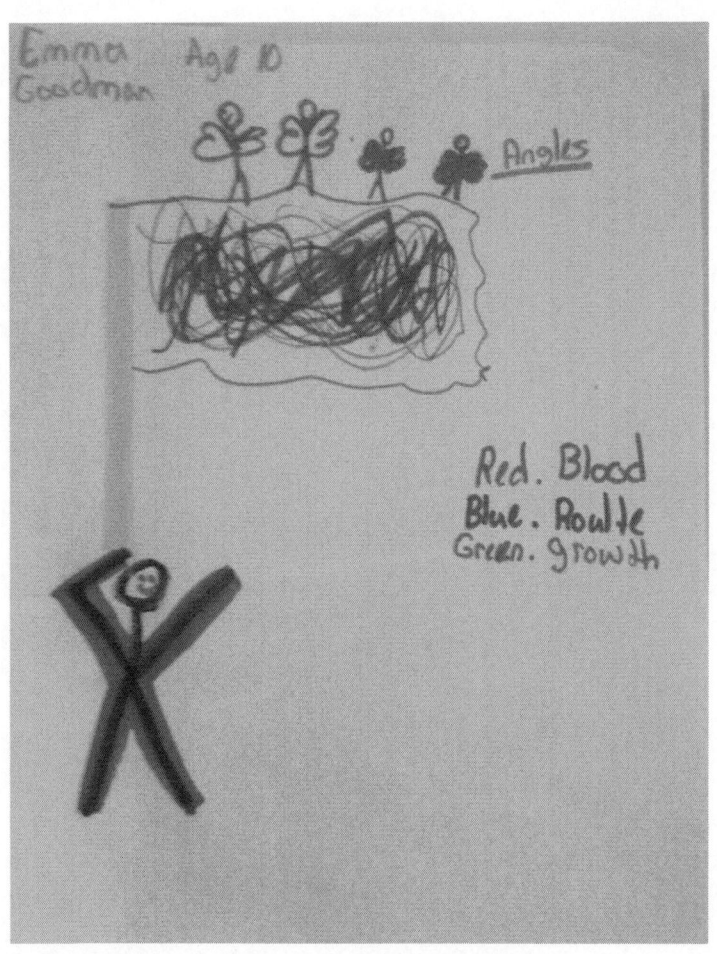

When we praise with our whole heart our enemies will be turned away by Gods presence. Ps 9:1-4

Our job is to praise the Lord. 1 Pet 2:9 Because He has already given us all we need. We just need to believe Him.

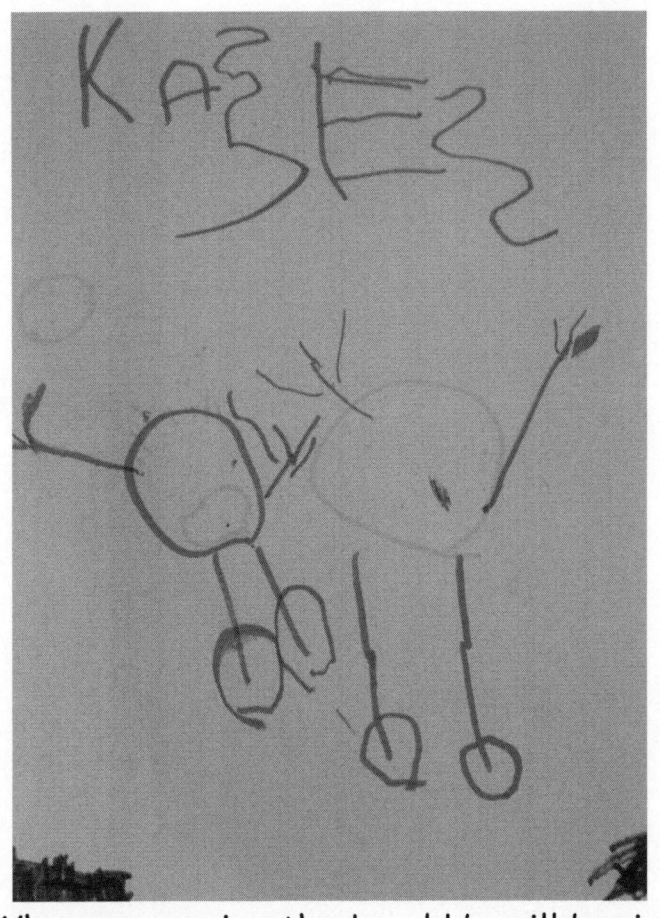

When you praise the Lord He will begin to heal people and set people free. through your prayers.

As you praise the Lord, He teaches you the Word and helps you understand the Bible.

One way you can praise God is to write a list of 5 things you really love. Then start thanking God for everything on your list.

When you start praising God He will come visit you because He wants to hear what you have to say about Him!

ABOUT THE AUTHOR

Robin Bremer is an ordained minister, who has appeared on the Tom Leding TV show "In God Your Will Succeed", and several radio shows. She is also a Comic Ventriloquist Motivational Speaker sharing "Keys to Working the Kingdom System". Her calling is to bring God's presence and Supernatural Power through the message of the KINGDOM of JOY and to set people free from a godless religion of "doing and works" into a personal, SUPERNATURAL relationship with Jesus Christ.

Robin has been a clown and ventriloquist for 22 years and ministers to both children and adults.

Blog: http://www.robinbremer.net contact Robin for guest appearances on TV, radio or for speaking engagements, retreats or events at RobinBremer@sbcglobal.net.

918-926-0707
Rt 2 Box 1936
Checotah, OK 74426

Other Books by Robin Bremer
Book Store: http://astore.amazon.com/kinlivforendt-20

Kingdom Living Series Vo. 1-3
Kingdom Living Bible Study Course Vol. 1-3
Pocket Study Guides Vol.1
80 Fact & Answers about Angles
Use Your Words
Ribbons The Clown Coloring Book

I pray that you are blessed by this book!

Robin Bremer

Printed in Great Britain
by Amazon